12 LAWS OF HUMANITY

12 Laws of Humanity

MICHELLE SMIC

Smic Life smiclife.com

Contents

Intro		1
1	We are judged by the measure in which we judge	4
2	We determine our emotions	10
3	The truth is constantly being revealed	14
4	People are good, intelligent, and reliable	18
5	Our feelings determine our priorities	22
6	Perseverance of priorities produces results	28
7	Fear leads to fear mongering	33

8	Shame leads to segregation	39
9	Pride leads to conformism	43
10	Working together bring harmony	48
11	Joy multiplies when it is shared	51
12	Generosity makes the world go around	55

Copyright © 2021 by Team Smic Pty Ltd
Qld AUSTRALIA
www.smiclife.com

All rights reserved. No part of this publication may be reproduced in any form, stored in a retrieval system, or transmitted in any form or by any means – for example by any electronic, recording, photocopying or mechanical means including information storage and retrieval systems, without the prior written permission of Team Smic Pty Ltd.

This publication is intended to provide helpful and informative material in regard to the subject matter. It is sold with the understanding that the Author and Team Smic Pty Ltd expressly disclaim responsibility for any adverse effects arising from the application or use of any advice or information contained in this publication.

This book is not intended as a substitute for medical advice from a qualified physician. The intent of this book is to provide general information in regard to the subject matter covered. Readers should consult their personal health professional before adopting any of the suggestions or be influenced by anything in this book. If medical advice or other expert help is needed, the services of an appropriate medical professional should be sought.

Cover & interior design by Michelle Smic

ISBN TP: 978-0-6451875-6-4
ISBN eBook: 978-0-6451875-5-7
FIRST EDITION, 2022

Intro

The twelve laws of humanity apply to us as a condition of being human. These are not rules that we have to adhere by to escape punishment. They are laws that we are bound by as a condition of being human, just like we are bound by the law of gravity by being on earth. Knowing these laws can help us to understand who we are, what we do and why we are here. While the knowledge found in this book has the power to change, it is only through application that understanding is found. There is no doubt in my mind that understanding what these laws are changes the way we live our lives. They aren't created for the judgment of others, but for the edification of ourselves and the compassion for others. We are able to understand people on a much better level and help others fight their fight as they help us fight our fight. This leads to the creation of sustainable communities and sustainable humanity by the gifts passed down the generations.

Life was not meant to be complicated; it doesn't have to be frustrating, depressing, or full of fear. Life was meant to be simple. It's a counterintuitive statement when we have been raised in a world that promotes and encourages followers and victims. In a world that promotes pride and self-love it may be hard to accept such information with an open and excited heart. I am not asking you to accept this information without understanding it, I am also not willing to justify myself or convince you that these laws are true. It is through the knowledge offered in this book that I'm asking you to observe and consider if these could be true. When we observe to gain clarity we may be tempted to instruct and share our knowledge, please don't as judgement can create bondage. Please instead offer the wisdom written in this book as knowledge. See knowledge to knowledge leads to submission, understanding to knowledge leads to confusion but wisdom to knowledge leads to clarity.

When we ask questions, we gain understanding. For this reason, I suggest that you ask a friend or family to come on this journey with you. Discussion and reflection will help everyone gain clarity of intensions and idols. I will guarantee that you will not agree with all the information or laws on your first experience. It will take time to understand and be able to fully comprehend and conceive these laws. These laws may be completely new to you, or you may have experienced them before, I ask that you give yourself and others permission to grow and learn. I ask you to give time to experience and understand what knowing these laws does to your life.

Chapter 1

We are judged by the measure in which we judge

Passing judgement on someone is what we can all do. It seems that while we are alive, we are unable to get away from it. Judging others can keep us safe, it can help us determine the value other see in us, and it can help us find our place and purpose in this world. The judgement we make of other people is important to help us determine what we value, what we want, and how we see this world. If we believe that all people are terrible and horrible and untrustworthy, and they don't deserve good things, then that is the measure in which we judge ourselves. Somewhere deep down we believe that we are terrible and horrible and untrustworthy and that we don't deserve to have anything that is good. The negative way this work is it can keep us in a rut or never-ending cycle of repeating past expectations. When we are unaware of this law, we can predict our future is going to be the same as our past because we have no other experience or exposure in which to judge the world. We can only predict or expect things to happen in the future as they have happened in the past. If we believe the things that happened in the past are bad, then we expect and predict that only bad things will happen in the future. When we choose to look deeper, and question to learn from the things that have happened in the past, we can see that good things have come out of them. When we can appreciate the good things that happen then our future will look much brighter. When we can see or allow ourselves to investigate, experience or comprehend those things that have happened in our past, we can see how they ended up saving us from something. If we can't see it yet, our story isn't over yet. We don't know the whole story; we can't control others through our opinions we can only control OUR future through our judgements. Our judgments of others reflect our judgement of ourselves. The things that have happened that we perceive as bad, actually created a point of change. The point of change may have been unexpected or unpleasant because it was uncomfortable, unfamiliar, or unpredictable, but we don't need to expect it to get worse.

Taking the time to understand why we make these judgments on other people; we can see that judgements come from an inability to justify the action. We can fail to look at our own actions that contributed to the change, this can lead to us blaming someone, or another change in our lives. Our minds are a powerful system that we may not see that our judgements of the past have power to embed themselves in our beliefs of what we expect out of life. When this happens, they have the power to disrupt our thoughts and can poison our views and assumptions about ourselves, our relationships, our community, and the way the world works.

When justification is our aim through judgment, we don't give ourselves grace to learn. Somewhere along the line we were all put down or mocked for not knowing something, resulting in this idea that we should have known it already. I see so often people make comments regretting that they have spent time learning. Somehow, we assume that we were born already knowing everything. We can see growth as a negative thing that makes us less of a person. When it actually, through learning makes us a better person.

No one is perfect and that's kind of the point. We don't know what perfection is or what a perfect person would look like. Each one of us would have a different version of what a perfect person would be. Your version would look vastly different to my version and another person's version could have a completely different set of ideas, morals, and concepts of which they perceive perfection. Who is right, who is wrong and who gets to decide which is which? We are all a version of ourselves and a product of the judgments we have made in the past. If we choose to judge others by the standard that we want to be judged, we find people that will show us the direction we want to go. When we judge others by this standard, we don't waste our time judging things we can't change, but rather changing ourselves by making positive changes to what we focus on.

When blame is our reason for judgment, we hand over the authority of our life to another person. We can see ourselves as powerless to change the outcome. We become victims of our own life, expecting someone else should have told us, or someone else has the answer or someone else will fix it for us. Each life is our own and our own responsibility. No one else can have real authority over our life. Every healthy person is busy taking charge of their own life. If someone is trying to take charge of our life, they won't be overseeing their own life. Feeling they need to take charge of someone else's life stems from the assumption that we can't take charge of our own life, this happens because they can't take charge of their life. They have generally given up their choices and authority to someone else and so assume that you need to and should do the same thing. It is the judgements that are made that determine our understanding of how the world functions.

Chapter 2

We determine our emotions

This is one of my favourite laws because it was the one that had the biggest breakthrough for me. I had been told that I had no say over my emotions, but when I discovered what emotions are, I discovered the contrary. If we choose a better future understanding our emotions are how we get there. We can never truly hide from, try to manipulate, or squash our emotions at any moment. Just as we have chosen our emotions over time, we can change our emotions over time. This is less about a single choice, but rather a repeated choosing and an intentional creation of a habit.

Emotions can be confusing, complicated, and complex, with an unlimited number of labels as well as the variations of interpretations. When I came to understand what makes up our emotions, it became straightforward to recognise my patterns of thoughts and feelings. Emotions are the label given to a feeling. For every feeling there are different thoughts, and because everyone has different thoughts and intentions, our interpretations of a label can be different again. For example, happy to one person can mean excited or full of energy, while to another it may mean a calm sense of relief. We can create many more emotions with our thoughts, and the comprehension of these, grow harder and more complicated with every moment.

Emotions broken down are the name we give a thought; and a feeling that we feel. We choose the thought or name but don't choose the feeling. Shakespeare asked "What's in a name? That which we call a rose by any other word would smell as sweet." The name or label of a feeling doesn't change the feeling, it can only affect our understanding of it. While there are so many labels there are only three contributing factors to our feelings, that is what we feel.

The only measures we can gauge are:
The level of tension in our body.
The level of energy in our feel, and
The level of openness we feel.

The level of tension is our body is the easiest to gauge and if we have ever had a good massage, we would know the difference between a tense or relaxed body.

The level of energy in our body is measured by our motivation or enthusiasm. Going to your favourite event or looking forward to an upcoming occasion, you will experience a higher level of energy than going to an event that you would rather not attend.

The level of openness is a little harder to explain, but when it's understood, it is hard to ignore. This comes down to our willingness to accept the situation we are in or be generous with what we have. We can either be curious about what is happening and how we can be part of what is around us or we become closed off and detach from other people, opportunities, or possibilities.

Chapter 3

The truth is constantly being revealed

As much as telling the truth can be hard in the moment, lying is never a good solution. When we avoid the truth there is a good chance, we will have to extend the propaganda to cover up our original untruth. We then have to continue telling lies, or continue the original lie, as we continue to not face the truth. We end up with a web of lies that we must remember, spending most of our brains compacity with hiding the truth. It only takes one slip up for the web of lies to be unravelled. We don't have to tell the truth, but the truth is always being revealed. Honouring the truth is about honouring trust. If we are caught lying, we break the trust in ourselves to determine the truth, and we all need trust to have sustainable relationships. When we lie and become untrustworthy to those that are important to us, and relationships start to break down. If the people weren't important to us, we wouldn't care what they thought and so we would tell the truth to save ourselves.

This law doesn't just work for lies though, it also works for who we are, what we are good at and what we know. If we set a habit or trend by lying about what we do, we will also lie about who we are. We can never know the entirety of who we are, as this also is constantly being revealed to us. When we look for what is being revealed to us, we are looking out for the truth, and we when this becomes a habit and a way of thinking, we will see the truth with ease. When we don't expect it to come, we avoid it until we end up slamming into it like a brick wall rather then gently putting on the breaks as we see it approaching. It can really hurt to hit a speed bump at full speed, no matter how small it may be. When we expect it and see it coming it is much easier to deal with, we can see it better in its entirety and it is a lot less painful.

The truth helps us to see what we value and what other people value. The greatest measure of truth is time. If we try a new fertiliser on a tree, the results are only seen through time, maybe only the next week, season, or year. If we believe a certain way of lying is better than another, it is only by time that we can tell. When we hold on to what we believe and make it more important than learning, we don't stop that truth from being revealed. We only increase the force that we will hit the bump in the road. No one can possibly know the complete truth; we can't see a big enough picture or comprehend enough to know the complete truth. We can only examine what we see, we all have information and beliefs, and it is through these beliefs that we see the world. When what we expect isn't what we see, there is information to be found and a truth to be revealed. We cannot ever know if what we believe is completely true. Even through the passage of time we will never completely understand how. All we have is our beliefs and that is all we will ever have. Our beliefs will always be a subsidiary of the truth. The truth cannot find its place in one person or in one idea, its only through time and community that the 'true' truth can be discovered.

Chapter 4

People are good, intelligent, and reliable

This is the first law about relationships, and a type of extension on the last. Some may argue that our current world is proof that this law is not true, but it is rather a reflection of our own beliefs. All people are governed by these laws, the belief or understanding of these laws doesn't change our capacity to abide by these laws. Just as we are governed by the laws of gravity, so too are we governed by these laws. Not believing that gravity exists does not make us float up in the air. All people are good at something and want to be better, but better at what is the question. We all value different things and this decides what we are good at. All people can see patterns and solve problems, to get to a goal or what they are working towards. Discovering what they are working towards is the key. All people take comfort and are familiar with something or somewhere. All people want to be accepted. No matter who we are or what we have said, we all want to feel accepted.

We put time and energy into what we value. If we don't value an object, we won't invest our money for it and if we don't value a skill, we won't invest our time in developing it. Our skills are the results of what we have valued more than other things to invest our time and energy into. If we value cooking, we invest our time into cooking, if we value relationships, we invest our time into building relationships. If we don't value the truth, we invest our time and energy into getting better at hiding who we really are. People are good, they want to be good and so invest their time in being good at what they value.

We all have a mind and although the physical size is similar, the capacity of our minds depends on what we fill it with. What we fill it with will determine our intellectual capacity. Some people spend their time studying and researching insects, others study and research plants and other people study and research to find the best ways to get away with lying. While the majority of the mind is trying to remember the web of lies so they don't get caught in it, there is no room left to study and research themselves, reasoning or the source of beliefs.

When we know ourselves and know what we value, we spend time with people who value the same things. When we are not sure what we value, we can spend our time with people who don't value us and spend our energy blaming them for not valuing the same things that we value. While looking at farmers, one values pastures, while another values cultivation, and even within that, one values orchids while another cropping. None is wrong, or bad, they are just different and provide variety of options for those who value their products.

It all comes down to this, we all want to be accepted and trusted. We try to get there through diverse ways, but the destination we all aim for remains the same. Success can be measured by a place where we can be who we are without fear of judgment. When we review the law of judgment, we know the way to get there is to see that people are all looking for the same thing, when we understand that we all value different things, we see that the paths we take to get there can be quite different.

Chapter 5

Our feelings determine our priorities

It is through our feelings that we make all our decisions. Our decisions are how we identify what we value the most compared to what we don't value. It is through our decisions that our feelings have developed, and we have established a way of thinking. The cycle of thoughts to feeling, new feelings to thoughts and new thoughts to feelings continues from the moment we receive knew information. How we receive this information is our decision. Our decision determines if we move towards tension or away from tension. The decision to hide from the truth moves towards tension while if we choose to accept or even consider the information as viable, we move away from tension. The next step is if we choose to implement the information, we consider moving towards more energy or our energy being put into something that doesn't give us energy. Whatever the outcome is, we receive greater understanding, either understanding the effects of the new information or confirming and understanding the original information on a greater level. The next decision in the cycle is whether we acceptance and are open to the next step of growth and the information leading to growth, or if we still seek control.

When we are offered or confronted with new information, we are presented with an idea of an unknown value of truth. If we choose to reject information without consideration, we choose to listen to our fear or the increased tension in our body. It is not the information that we are afraid of, but the unknown. We really could not know the effects of this information at the first encounter, all we can do is consider it. It is never the messenger that we hate or fear but rather the information that they bring or the actions that they value. When we fear the unknown, we are not open to the truth. If someone brings us something that looks like an answer, we can want to trust them, think about it logically and do all the calculations and we may see that there is no other choice, but our tension level will be the indicator. There is always another choice, but what we can't see is something that we've never experienced, or the unknown. We are not afraid of information because deep down we know that information alone cannot hurt or harm us. Once evaluated we can choose to reject the information and life goes on as before, or we accept the information and our life changes, or we become curious about where it came from or where it may lead.

During this process it is important to remember that all information comes from opinions. There is no true measure in which we can decipher an absolute truth. It is only through our feelings and decisions that we create the illusion of facts. All our feelings and decisions have given us experience or exposure to different information and environments. By taking the information and making the relevant changes in our lives, that information can now have a positive effect, but it's important to remember that our minds compacity is full. If we are willing to decide and accept or decline information, we have reached a level of mental discipline that allows us to process questions. We are no longer looking to just fill a void in our minds like children, but a search for constructive perceptions. Our minds capacity is expanded when we consider updated or exchanging information of greater value compared to the value of our existing thoughts. On this consideration we will discover what thought process the latest information will replace. What made a large difference in my life and the lives of my clients is understanding that the point of friction happens close to the point of replacement. When we understand what is happening the process is less scary and becomes like walking a well-known path. When we accept a new way of doing things, we need to give up our old way of doing it. Processing new information can be harder if we think we are stepping into the unknown rather than discovering the truth of what always was. We do have to let go of the things from the past, things that once brought us comfort. If we find that over time the new way doesn't work, we always have the option of moving onto another way.

Accepting new information isn't about copying someone else's life. It is about taking the information we're given as an example to discover a new way. It seems to be that when we receive information that is new and different, it opens our eyes to the possibilities. It is through these possibilities that we find ourselves inventing and expanding on what we are given. It is not about becoming cookie cutters of each other, always trying to fit into a mould or others expectation of us, but what the information exposes us to. It is opening our eyes to experience something new and growing through it so we can then share our experience with others.

It's not about their way, or my way but through these we can discover our own way.

Chapter 6

Perseverance of priorities produces results

No matter what you are doing, if you stick with it long enough, you will get there. Rome wasn't built in a day, and we weren't born knowing everything. Things take time because things need to grow. If we are not growing, we are decaying. If we have a desire for something and don't have it, it's because we haven't valued it long enough to allow it to grow or we have valued something else more. It's not because we don't deserve it or we can't have it, it is usually because we need to grow into it.

Knowledge is not a key to getting what we desire, and neither is understanding. It's the passionate pursuit of our purpose over time that creates results. For example, a seed will sprout with water; it will grow with fertiliser, but it will not bear fruit without light. The information written in this book is not new information to me. This information was revealed to me over time, what I failed to understand was its value. Now I have the privilege of seeing the effect this has on people, I see the good changes, not only in their relationships but their outlook on life. Knowledge is not the point of life; a life cannot be lived without growth. When we water a plant, the point is not to water it, but we need to water it so it will grow. We want the plant to grow so that it will fruit, or blossom, we do not want the plant to grow so we can continue to water it. Water is like knowledge in the way that too much can cause a tree to drown, too little and the tree is starved of what it needs to survive. The same amount of water that can drown a tree can be absorbed by it if it is given the time to grow while absorbing the information through the passage of time.

Persevering is the result of consistently having the same priorities long enough for us to grow into the person who has it. When we continue to preserver with our priorities, we may need to discover every way that doesn't work before we find the way that does. This isn't to be despised but celebrated because it is how we know the value of our properties. If our priorities are not worth pursuing then we would not value it if we already had it, or we could have had it and didn't value it enough to keep it. This is a process of absorbing knowledge. We are able to receive knowledge as it comes and don't drown ourselves with the accumulation of information that has no effect on our life. When we process information as it comes, we don't become overwhelmed by information and choices, but grow sustainably and continuously.

The other option is that other people need

time to grow into the knowledge we share. It's like children knowing how to drive the car before they can touch the pedals. They may know, or think they know but without ever having done it on their own, for their own, how can they really know if they do know? Sometimes we are ready and willing to share information from our growth, but the information causes people to conform because it provides a black and white view. But wisdom allows people to not value the information we value and give them permission to grow in a different way from how we have grown. It's not about the information but the understanding, understanding takes different paths for all people.

Our priorities are our most significant measure of perseverance. Having sustainable priorities makes perseverance a more naturally occurring part of our life. If we struggle with perseverance, we struggle with our priorities. If looks become our greatest single priority, greater then family, friends, work, food, or pleasure, then perseverance isn't sustainable. In a similar way if pleasure becomes our greatest priority, it can take the place of friends, family, work, food or health. Whatever we have chosen to value, that is our priority. Whatever we choose to continually value is what we have in our life.

When we have conflicting priorities, we spend all our energy fighting against ourselves and end up getting nowhere. We don't seem to have any results but confusion and lack of energy. Take note and know the priorities that we are pursuing and remind ourselves often of them. Taking notes of distractions or other priorities that pull us away or contradict the ability to persevere the greater priority will give clarity on the real or persistent priorities and not just the ones we take note of. Being super clear about the priorities we pursue will allow us to persevere without strain or strife.

Chapter 7

Fear leads to fear mongering

Fear is an emotion that most commonly stems from the feeling of high tension in the body. Anxiety, pressure, worry, horror, and stress all show up as tension in our body. Please remember that these are emotions that are open to interpretation due to the unique label that each one of us will give them.

It's important to know our enemies, because if we don't know our enemies, we can end up fighting off the very things that were there to help us. We don't need to fight against people and never have. When we see people as our enemy, we forget that everyone is fighting the same battle in our minds. Some are winning more often than other, some don't know who they are fighting so come out swinging, and some have given up altogether, after fighting for years without a rest.

It is our own fears we are fighting. Fear of not being accepted, fear of running out of time or fear of being hurt or our physical death. I don't know of anything we can fear that doesn't come under one of those categories. When others tell us to be fearful, they help us to see their fears. We don't have to take these on as our fear, and we can't fight their fear for them. The only thing left to do is shine our light for them so that they may see, it must be their choice to accept information and grow.

Fear of hurt and physical death can also be a fear of lack or FOMO. A fear that we will lose security, lose money, lose a house, feel cold, feel hungry, not have a car and many more. All these fears can be brought back to a physical fear. Fear of something going 'wrong' in the physical world. Fear of death can come under here if we are afraid our children or partner won't be looked after. It is a physical fear.

Fear of running out of time can get us running around trying to get everything done but finding we often don't have the energy to do it. This is also about being seen as enough. What is enough? What if we had enough, what would that look like? Most of the time we have enough air to breath, water to drink and nourishment to survive. What we sometimes forget through this fear is that if we have those things, we are enough to do anything else with the right amount of time. If we don't have enough of anything, time is the passage we take to attain it. We have exactly enough time here on earth to do what we need to do, because the moment we are no longer on this earth, we no longer need to do the things we thought we did. I have found spending our time learning and growing is the most effective way to spend our time. It allows us to move with changing circumstances and flow into life. This time is what we can't give to the next generation. We can save our money and give it as a lump sum, but the value of the money decreases if we do. When we value the time, we have to grow, we pass on that growth to the next generation so that they can grow from there.

Fear of the not being accepted may have been my biggest fear of all. It is the one that has the most facets because on consideration of what makes us accepted and who accepts us. I feel the other two fears can in some ways be linked to this fear of not being accepted. We all need love and acceptance; it is the biggest driving force I see in people. It can make us get out of the morning, go to work, the party, dress up, dress down, buy that car, buy that house. It is not the only reason but it can be the reason so many people do the same thing day in and day out. Its why social media is a booming industry, and why we can search for the acknowledgment or shares.

I would like to estimate that fear is the main reason for about ninety percent of the industries in today's economy. When you picture the number of industries that have established themselves in the last two hundred years, we can see that they do not fill our needs, but our want for acceptance. I am not even suggesting that progress is bad, but where are we going? People say the world is moving ahead and we live in a progressive time, but in what direction? When we look at the things that we don't need for survival, like TVs, Cars, and electronics we are seeing major changes and developments. Is this sustainable? When we look at the things we need to live sustainably like food, shelter, and water, are we moving in a positive direction? Our fear driven culture may have us focused on producing the things that will not lead to the sustainability of life.

Let us be real. Our fear of not being accepted has us putting on faces, striving to find our tribe and trying to manage people's perception of us rather than changing ourselves. One of these ways are exhausting, and the other is freeing. How accepted can we truly be if no one knows who we really are? It is easy to say and ask but wouldn't it be easier for people to accept us if we were ourselves? Wouldn't it be easier to accept people if we knew they were not driven by fear?

Chapter 8

Shame leads to segregation

Shame is a feeling of low energy in our body. It is depression, sadness, despair, grief, and sorrow are all emotions that can be used to explain the feeling of low energy. The feeling of low energy is not to be confused with peace which is a feeling of low tension. While at the first glance low tension and low energy may feel the same, but with genuine investigating and reflection, we can all come to know the difference between the two. Rest comes from knowing everything is going to be all right. Shame comes from believing the energy we use has no effect on the world or that no matter what we do, things cannot change for the better.

When we don't feel we have the ability to change, we are held captive by not have a clear positive purpose in life. We feel unworthy and pull away from people when we have depleted energy. We don't invest our energy in anything that will give us energy because we start to believe that it is all a waste of time and energy. Shame comes when we spend our energy trying to hide what we have done, when we push away new positive information under the illusion of offence or when we hold onto old information that is keeping us captive.

When we try to hide instead of being willing to learn from what we did, we spend our energy on something that will take and continue to use our energy. When we invest our energy in learning, we continue to expand the energy we have, and we can exchange energy through the process of growth. Growth is an important part of life because things are always changing. Growth is change in a positive direction, while not growing means we are decaying and moving in a negative direction.

New information is the greatest gift we can be given. People are destroyed because of lack of knowledge, so our only way to survive is to receive knowledge. This doesn't mean we have to accept it all, but rather receive it. If it has no effect on us, we can let it go, but if the new knowledge creates a change in our feelings, it is time to make a change to our knowledge. Offence is how we know the information has an element of truth. If I said a flower was blue when it was clearly yellow, you would think there is something wrong with me. But if I was to say it was light orange, you may consider my view and question your original thought.

No bad thing will come from offence but more offence if we decide we don't want to change. Personal change, mental discipline or growth is the remedy to not being offended. Remember we are not fighting people, so if 'someone' offends us, it is not by them but by the information they have given us that causes offence. We are not fighting them but fighting to accept or dismiss the information they have given us as their belief. The battle is in our mind between what we thought was true and what we have now been given to consider as true.

Old information can be hard to let go of as it can give us comfort or the illusion of control. Old information and ways of doing things can feel safe, secure, and familiar. It can also hold us in great pain and have us expecting something that on some level we know is not a possibility. It has the potential to keep us in limbo, growing in shame but still stuck in a never-ending hamster wheel of using up our energy.

Chapter 9

Pride leads to conformism

We may have been told that pride is a good thing, by people saying things like "Be proud of yourself," or "be proud of what you've done," but when we understand the implications of pride, we may start to look at pride a little differently. I believe pride has been encourages on many occasions with good intention but not with the complete understanding of the results it produces.

Conformism is the acceptance of the actions or principle that we can only come together with those who think or do the same as us. It is when we believe that everyone should fit into a box or under a label. It is believing that everyone needs to conform to a certain type of behaviour, or belief system otherwise they are 'wrong'. Believing there is only one right and one wrong for everyone will cause us to try to figure out which is which. The only opinion we have comes from a screwed viewpoint, and this is what we trust to determine what is right and wrong is from our own experiences and exposures. This justifying our own life is measuring or judging people according to our own path or destination. It can make us feel right but it never gives us the opportunity to learn.

This is the place we all must make our hardest choice. The law, 'pride leads to conformism' is a law and doesn't change. What can change is if we see pride and conformism as a positive thing or a negative thing. This choice comes down to this, are you going to be the one who determines what's right and wrong in the world and for other people or are you going to be the one who determines what is right and wrong in our own mind and our own actions. The ease of this decision comes when we know the one we can control and one we cannot.

Pride is a feeling of completeness, the finality of an achievement or the righteousness of our beliefs. It is when we believe we have nothing else to learn. Things are always changing and will always be changing. When we expect other people to change to our personal standard, judgment, or system of belief we become exhausted trying to change something we can't. When we invest that same energy in changing ourselves, our standard and our belief system, we all experience positive growth through new experiences and exposures. This leads to positive change and sustainable relationships.

When we choose to be proud, we take one moment of our lives and place it as more important than any other time. We define our life by one aspect of it. There was a time when we all knew nothing, and everything we have learnt we have learnt through people and interactions with people. Whenever we have thought that we 'made it,' we realise there is another day, another moment, and another opportunity we haven't yet experienced. Looking at our life as a destination will never sustain life as we will always be looking for a resting place, in someone, something or in a destination. All we have in life is this breath and this moment. Nothing is guaranteed, not another day, hour, or opportunity. The only opportunity we have is to change ourselves, by changing ourselves we are changing the world because we are part of the world.

Some may want to choose conformism, which is each person's choice. Conformism can help us understand and make sense of the world. It can make us feel safe, avoid change and therefore avoid unfamiliar and unpredictable situations. This can be an asset to some. The only reason this can be an asset is if our underlying intention is to control people and situations to get to our destination. If we all ended up at the same place and destination it would be awfully crowded and boring. Everyone would be predictable, and everyone would be battling for the top spot. The only destination we will all end up at is death, while we strive to get there we will, but this would not be a sustainable way to live.

We all have our own paths, that intertwine, align with, and join other people's paths. When we search for that destination, we can live with what I call 'strangled hope.' This is when we are striving to make it to a destination or objective and not living the life we are given now. We have hope for a better future, an idea or plan to get us there, but it is at the sacrifice of our life today.

Chapter 10

Working together bring harmony

This law makes perfect sense to me, but it seems to be the one I forget the easiest. We may have heard the sayings, 'Many hands make light work,' 'There is no 'I' in team' "Alone we can do little, together we can do much" (Helen Keller) or "It takes a village to raise a child", but do we live it?

Many people working towards one goal is bound to bring results faster and easier than one working against the rest. The missing link to harmony maybe that the goal we want to achieve is not united. If we come together and want to work together but it is just not working, we have to ask, has the common goal been set, are we all heading in the same direction? The world at this stage seems to be divided, everyone is working towards their own goals and the world is left in destitution. Everyone is pulling away from a central purpose and pulling away from each other.

If we choose to work against the people around us or against the goal that they are working towards, it causes tension. It can cause tension for both parties but more so for the party who is outnumbered or working against the greater good of the generations.

When we recognise and can appreciate the assertiveness of other people, we can ask them to join the common goal. The common goal that we all work towards needs to be for the benefit of everyone, that is everyone living, everyone who has already passed and those who are yet to be born. The only and most important goal that I can think of is the sustainability of humanity. Everyone has a role to play is this, simply by being born we are taking part in the sustainability of humanity. We are already a benefit from here, what every we do, we can do for the good of all or for the temporary pleasure of ourselves. One is sustainable, one is not.

We can look at the example of the people who have gone before us, every generation this far has succeeded in the sustainable growth of humanity. If the growth or needs of an individual is held above the needs of humanity, then humanity is moving towards an unsustainable future. It is only when we are willing to lay down our own beliefs and pleasures for the prosperity of the human race that our lives will truly be productive.

Chapter 11

Joy multiplies when it is shared

Joy is a precious gift we are given, but it only comes through those around us. While the sustainability of humanity is important to our existence, without joy and fellowship there is no energy for us. Our joy is a high energy level, and a high energy level is our joy. Without energy we have no food, no purpose, and no relationship. It is through our food, purpose, and relationships that we receive our energy.

When we sow a seed, we have food. When we sow into our talents, we receive purpose and when we sow into others, we have relationships. It is only when we share what we have that it has the opportunity to grow. If we hold onto our seed, hide our talents, or run from people, they will soon turn to poison in our lives.

If we think of the last time, we had a good laugh or remarked that we were happy it was in the presence of someone, or in relation to someone. That person did not make us happy, and we did not make the other person happy, but it is through the relationship, the shared experiences, and shared goals that we find our greatest connections and share our greatest joy.

Laughter is infections because it speaks to the deepest part of our being. It speaks to a part that is not occupied by our mind or thoughts, but to our core. Our core, our spirit or heart is where our deepest desires are found, grow and flourish. These desires are not pleasures and need to be sustainable desires, to produce sustainable joy. Unsustainable desires bring unsustainable pleasure. Pleasure is the result of selfish desires with unsustainable intentions.

These unsustainable intentions work against the greater good and the sustainability of humanity.

Intentions of self-protection, self-preservation or self-promotion work against the sustainability of humanity and of lasting joy, and sustainable energy.

Intentions of sustaining life and humility will sow into things that promote growth in all areas. The world can sustain more life than our calculations can predict. The life that the world sustains grows into positive energy, community living and provides more opportunities to produce more life. The life we need to focus on preserving is the human life, as a bee is irreplaceable in pollinating flower, so humans are in working the earth.

When we share our ideas with the right intention, people will grow, whether the information is correct or not. People will grow because it will start the conversation to discover what is the truth being revealed. It is through the sharing, and growing process that positive energy is exchanged and expands. Just like laughter and just like joy, our energy grows the more we share.

Chapter 12

Generosity makes the world go around

This is the final law and the one that is evident in every other law. We came into this world with nothing. Our parents gave us all that we have, whether they gave a lot or a little is not the point as much as they gave. No one would be here if we didn't have parents who gave us life. After they gave us life, they gave us opportunities, and after opportunities we receive freedom. With the freedom of choice comes the opportunity to be generous ourselves.

These positive cycles of generosity are

extraordinary satisfying when it is fulfilled. The momentum increases as growth is easy, leading to further prosperity and further growth. We cannot produce food if we don't sow the seed. We don't have energy if we don't first sow food into our bodies. We don't have a reason for food if we don't sow into the next generation.

This cycle is found in all positive areas of life.
Food = energy = purpose = food production.
Knowledge = growth = sharing = knowledge
Opportunities = action= relationships = opportunities
Growth = healing = trimming = growth

It is only through the process of acceptance that this cycle can be beneficial. All cycle can be broken or changed at any time, which is good news because these cycles are also present with the negative things of life also.

Negative cycles also exist.
Shame = regret = hiding = shame
Hate = control = anger = hate
Fear = justification = loneliness = fear

Our life always works in a cycle, any area we are generous in is the area that we receive in. The cycle cannot and will not progress if the previous steps are not taken, the longer we spend in a point on the positive cycle, the easier it is to slide into the negative.

When we want to take all we can from the world we will receive both positive and shame, hate and fear. When our time comes to leave this world, we give all we have. We cannot take anything with us and so our only options are to gift it or let it decay. Everything in this life stays in this life, so it is only by gifting what we can that we will truly have a life well lived. A life that took from the previous generation to sow what positive it could into the generations yet to come.

Thank you for taking the time to read this book and consider another point of view. This book is only a snapshot of the possibilities understanding these laws can have on a person, their relationships and goals and ambition for their life. These laws are not an asset until they have been understood to the point of complete implementation. If you would like more information about these laws and their effects, please check out 'Thinking for Yourself', 'The Pursuit of Patience', 'An Appetite of Appreciation' or one of the SMIC Life Seminars found on smiclife.com. Or take the time to investigate and understand them through your own life and experiences.

www.ingramcontent.com/pod-product-compliance
Lightning Source LLC
Chambersburg PA
CBHW071842290426
44109CB00017B/1903